# Starting A Foreclosure Cleanup-Property Preservation Business

Elider Desir

ISBN:1461148529
ISBN-13:9781461148524

## DEDICATION

A special dedication goes out to my daughter Daliyah. You have giving me the strength, motivation and the passion to continue every day, daddy loves you!

# CONTENTS

# ACKNOWLEDGMENTS

The author would like to thank his business partner Marie Edmond and Stephania Evens. Also like to thank my mentors, Julian Franco, Than Merrill and Preston Ely.

# 1 WHAT IS PROPERTY PRESERVATION?

Property Preservation is a term that the banks and asset management companies call vendors that repair and maintain their foreclosed properties.

## Who can perform Property Preservation services?

Contractors
Landscapers
Handyman
Plumbers
HVAC Contractors
Carpenters
Electricians
Trash Hauling Companies
Demolition Contractors
Painters
Carpet & Flooring Companies
House Cleaning Services
Pool Contractors
Roofing Companies
Drywall Contractors
Glass & Window Repair Companies
Locksmiths
Home Inspectors
Hazardous Material Removal
Automobile Removal Service
Tile companies
And anyone wanting to start this type of business!!!

**Here are some of the basic requirements you will need before you begin your Foreclosure Cleanup-Property Preservation business.**
**General Requirements for Property Preservation Vendors:**

- Maintain a General Liability insurance policy with a minimum coverage of $500,000 to $1,000,000

- Maintain Errors & Omissions insurance coverage in the amount of $1,000,000
- Maintain Auto Insurance (if applicable) Some vendors use rental trucks to start out to minimize costs
- Add client as an additionally insured under all liability policies
- Supply client with copy of the insurance certificate that shows they have been added to the policy
- Insurance renewals must be provided to the client
- Provide any required business licenses or miscellaneous licenses as needed (ex. Contractor's license)
- Insurance certificate must provide a minimum of 30 days' notice of cancellation or non-renewal stating that your company is not required to carry workers compensation
- Must supply federal taxpayer identification number or social security number
- Must be thoroughly familiar with FHA, VA, and HUD specifications as they relate to your area of coverage geographically
- Present a copy of a valid driver's license
- Must have all necessary office and field equipment necessary for timely completion of assignments
- A website

Most banks will require you to upload a copy of your liability insurance, a signed W-9 form, a copy of your Business License before they will accept you as a vendor.

All banks pay Property Preservation vendors as independent contractors. This is why they will need a signed W-9 form on file with the bank or asset management company.

# 2 TOOLS NEEDED

**The following are technological tools you will need to perform Foreclosure Cleanup-Property Preservation Services:**
Internet Connection
Cell Phone (preferably with internet and texting capabilities)
E-mail
Website
Digital camera
Answering machine
Fax machine
Scanner
Wireless Service for Cell Phone (optional); But it does allow you to receive your work orders from anywhere you are
Paper
Pen
Your work order papers regarding the current property
The banks contact phone number or Real estate agents phone number to contact

**What services can Property Preservation vendors and contractors perform?**
Initial securing of properties (Rekey or board up windows)
Install Lockboxes
Winterization
Bi-Weekly or Monthly lawn maintenance (Depending upon the geographical area of the property)
Eviction/move-out assistance
REO trash-outs and debris removal
Repairs as needed on a property by property basis
Pool Maintenance & Repair
Automobile removal
Hazardous Waste Removal
Install new or repair flooring (as needed)
Replace or repair windows (as needed)
And many more.....

**We want you to success and getting started properly is one of the keys to success! So let's get started!!**

# 3 BUSINESS START-UP

**Naming your business:**  You are going to have to decide on a name for your new business.  I highly recommend it state something regarding your new business and the services you offer.  This way it will be easy for the asset managers and reo agents to remember your company, thus increasing the amount of work you will get from them.

If you have not gotten your business license, your employer identification number, or set up your business type (sole proprietor, partnership, C Corporation, LLC, or S Corporation) yet-go back to www.listbankrepos.com and scroll towards the bottom of the home page; there is an ad where they can assist you with your corporation or any other entity type, as well as filing your employer identification number and getting your business license, all in one place and they are very quick about getting you up and running right away!
Some businesses can be formed and started within 3 business days or less.

**General Liability Insurance:**  Next, you are going to want to start receiving quotes for general liability insurance and worker's compensation insurance to decide which company will offer you the best insurance for the best price.  You will need worker's compensation insurance if you will be having employees also, if you are having family members work with you in your business-generally you do need workman's compensation insurance.  Check with your local state regarding their specific rules.  Generally, most banks require a $1,000,000 policy, this is the standard.

**Website:** You will definitely want to have a website in this business.  The REO asset managers and reo agents in this business will feel you are very professional with your own website and this is a must have in this business.  Once you have your website up and running, make sure to submit it to all the search engines so your website can be found.  Many places charge for these services.

**Purchasing Your Tools And Supplies:**  Next, you will want to start purchasing your items needed for your new business if you do not have them already.  There are some must have in this business such as a digital camera, cell phone, internet connection.

Other items that will be needed are a scanner, most banks prefer you to upload your invoices to their website and you will need to scan them and upload them.

So Let's Get Going!

# 4 MARKETING YOUR BUSINESS

The next step you will need to take is to start signing up with all the banks and asset management companies. Start with the Property Preservation contact list and begin signing up with all the website links. The banks and asset management companies will only speak to vendors once you have been accepted to work for them. Go to the list at the end of this training guide and start signing up with all of these companies. When you sign up, make sure to completely finish your profile with each one and take the time to enter ALL zip codes you are willing to work, this is how they assign the work orders is by the zip code of the property that has foreclosed on, if you are not listed in a certain zip code, you will not be considered for that property. Always add your photo or business logo (if you have one), but make sure to definitely have your photo in all of your profiles, asset managers love to associate a face with a name and this helps them remember you and your company better and to search for you when the properties come available. This highly increases the amount of work orders you will receive.

**Signing Up With The Banks & Asset Management Companies:** This is when you will need to usually upload your business license, signed W-9 form, a copy of your driver's license, and a current copy of your liability insurance for the bank to have on file. Most banks and asset management companies will not release any payments for work performed without these items.
Make sure that you also take the time to enter all zip codes that you would like to work in, it does take time, but this is how they assign the work orders for each property, by the vendors listed in those areas. Another great place to get new business is from the REO agents in your area. One great avenue of advertising is sending flyers to the local real estate offices advertising your Property Preservation services. Also sending emails to the REO agents in your area with a flyer attached is another fantastic way to build new business, because REO agents are almost always logged on to the internet as this is there they receive their work orders from the banks.
They are very busy so do not give up on them, usually it will take repeated emails and contacts with them before they will use your services.
It is highly suggested to have a website advertising your Property Preservation services too; it is a must have in this business and it shows

that your business is much more reputable to both the banks and to the REO agents highly increasing your opportunities for the work orders! Other great networking websites to help connect with your REO real estate agents:  Set up a Facebook, MySpace, and twitter accounts and advertise your services and connect with realtors and reo agents in your immediate area:

www.facebook.com

www.myspace.com

www.twitter.com

Many professionals are on twitter.  Also, you want to check your fico score if you will be applying for credit cards or getting any to start your business.  It is always a good idea to know and improve your credit.  We provided a discount for you to get your credit reports.

**Here are some additional great networking places to try to locate REO agents in your area:**

www.reomac.com

www.reonetwork.com

www.reoagents.net

www.reoassign.com

www.assignreo.com

www.reoallstars.com

www.nrba.com

www.reobroker.net

www.reomagazine.com

www.4reobrokers.com

# 5 HOW YOU WILL RECEIVE PAYMENTS

First and foremost, all banks and REO Asset Management companies pay at slightly different rates, however we will list the most general guidelines and what they will pay. Majority of the banks follow the HUD and VA guidelines for maximum amount that they will reimburse for your services. And yes, I did say reimburse. You will need to have some money set aside as most banks and asset management companies reimburse your costs of service approximately 30 to 45 days upon completion of your work performed. For people starting this business that have limited funds to begin with, one suggestion is to lease or rent your trucks that you will use to perform the work. Most banks that you will receive work from come with a complete list of their requirements once you have become accepted by that bank or asset management company. So, once you become accepted, please follow each banks or asset management companies set of rules for processing your payments. This is just a brief guideline of how it will work.

Generally, you will receive your work order or bid request via email or from the real estate agent you are working with. Most of the time you will be required to go out to the property and submit a bid for the work that they are requesting from you and all property photos to support the bid first before you will be awarded the work. The bank or realtor usually will also provide a form required to be submitted to the bank upon completion of your work after your initial bid has been accepted for you to be reimbursed for completed work. So, you will want someone knowledgeable to be in charge of your billing and accounts receivables. Once the work has been completed and your invoice has been submitted to the bank, it usually takes approximately 30 to 45 days to receive your payment.
If you are being paid by the realtor directly, you will need to establish when you will be paid with them directly. I highly recommend setting this up before any work is completed.

Once you receive your work order or bid request, you will need to go out to the property and take photos and create a bid estimate for your proposed work to be performed.

All banks and asset management companies require photos to back to your bid request, they all require before work photos and after completed work photos of the property in order to be reimbursed.

Once you have completed your initial bid and taken your photos, you will either upload them into the bank or asset management companies' site or email them directly to the realtor and they will upload them depending on who you are working for.

# 6 MARKET YOUR BUSINESS

This guide will teach you how to become a top internet marketer for your foreclosure cleanup property preservation business. Learn how to showcase your business services on twitter, Facebook, MySpace, and other social networks, how to get your website increased in Google and the search engines, place free classified ads advertising your services, submit free article submissions promoting you and your website, blogs and so much more...

Nearly 95% of real estate business owners across the US have a website, but less than 5% of real estate business owners actually get valuable leads from their website or get their website found in the search engines. You will learn about SEO (Search Engine Optimization) and how this will make your REO Agents and REO Asset Managers find your website. It's a must have to have a website in the real estate profession, but the best website does you no good if your website can not be found!!!

Learn valuable tools to get found on Google, yahoo, Bing, AOL, and other search engines so REO Agents & REO Asset Managers can find you today! Learn how to create blogs to promote people to your website and learn about your services. Find places to place free ads offering your services. Use craigslist to promote your services, too. Join valuable social networks and connect with other Real Estate agents and Top Asset Management Personnel. Make videos and upload them onto YouTube, MySpace, and more to promote your services. Install Google analytics to track how many visitors are coming to your website and where they are coming from!

Turn your website into a lead generating tool today! And grow your Foreclosure Cleaning Business Today! This will help you get more Foreclosure Cleaning-Property Preservation Contracts.

Summary of Topics to be Covered in the Marketing Section:

1. SEO (Search Engine Optimization) Learn tools to adjust your website to be found easier in Google and the search engines
2. Submit your website to the search engines to be found

3. Using Twitter to becoming a networking powerhouse for you & your website
4. Using Facebook to generate more clients and connect with others to offer your services
5. Placing free ads offering your services and sending them to your website
6. Blogs-Blogging is an excellent way to promote you and your business and to send many people to your website
7. Place free ads on Craigslist offering your services
8. Write free articles about what you have to offer and interesting things about your community to drive people to your website
9. Install an auto-responder if you don't have one for your emails so people get an instant response once they have visited your website
10. Join Industry networks & network with others in your community
11. Create videos of you and your services and place them on YouTube, MySpace, Facebook, and more sending people to your website
12. Install Google analytics so you can track the amount of people visiting your website and where they found you from
13. Register with REO Agent Directories so they can locate you to use your services

**SEO (Search Engine Optimization) and Why You Need It!**

What is search engine optimization?

Search engine optimization is the process of making a website and its content highly relevant for both search engines and searchers. SEO includes technical tasks to make it easier for search engines to find and index a site for the appropriate keywords, as well as marketing-focused tasks to make a site more appealing to users.

It sounds very technical, but there are some basics that anyone with a website can do to increase your websites ability to show up in the search engines. You want to show up in the search engines so your potential customers can find you!

The Internet has profoundly transformed the way people learn about and shop for products. Ten years ago, companies reach their consumers through trade shows, print advertising, and other traditional marketing methods. Today, consumers start their shopping experience by looking on the Internet, in the search engines, the blogosphere, and social media sites. In order to remain competitive, businesses' websites need to be found online by the consumers already searching for the products and services that you sell.

Businesses must get found online by the consumers searching for their products and services in the search engines, blogosphere and social media.

## There are two kinds of search results:
## Paid results and organic (or natural) results

Paid results are those listings that require a fee for the search engines to list their link for particular keywords. The most widely used form of paid listing is Pay Per Click (PPC), where you pay each time someone clicks on the link in your advertisement. The price increases with the competitiveness of the keyword.

Organic results are gathered by search engines' web crawlers and ranked according to relevance to search terms. This relevance is calculated by criteria such as extent of keyword match and number of links into that website. Ranking in the organic search results is better because not only is it FREE, but research shows that people click on the organic results 75% of the time and paid results only 25% of the time.

Google and the other search engines rank websites in search engine pages according to relevance to the search terms. This relevance is calculated by looking at both on-page factors such as the content on your site and off-page factors in the form of inbound links to your website off-page factors are the biggest influencers in your website's ranking in search engine results.

**Find Keywords**
**STEP 1:** Pick your keywords for your website

Search Volume – Given two different keyword phrases, optimize for the one with the larger number of searches.

Relevance – Choose keywords that your target market is using to describe and search for your products and services.

Difficulty or Competition – Consider your chances for ranking on the first page of Google for that keyword phrase. Look at the sites ranked in those first 10 slots, their authority and relevance to search terms, and gage if you will be able to overtake them to secure a spot on that first page.

**STEP 2:** On-Page SEO
Place keywords in the page title, URL, headings, and page text. This definitely helps your website get indexed better in the search engines!!

Optimize your page description for maximum click through rate when your site ranks in Google searches.

Place keywords in other "invisible" places on your site, including meta-keyword tags and alt-text on images.

**STEP 3:** Off-Page SEO
Build more inbound links from other sites into yours. Each link serves as a recommendation or a reference to tell the search engines that your site is a quality site.

Build more links within context, i.e. those with valuable keywords in the link anchor text (the text that is hyperlinked to your site). Link anchor text provides context for the search engines to understand what your site is about.

Build more links from trusted websites. Just as references from well-respected friends and experts offer more value, so do links from trusted and well-respected websites.

Link-building tips:

Submit your website to directories like Yahoo! Directory and Business.com

Communicate with others in your industry through blogs and other social media

Create compelling tools (Such as an interesting calculator) and content (via a blog, for example)

**STEP 4:** Measure & Analyze
Track number of inbound links, keyword rank over time and compared to competition.

Measure real business results: number of visitors, leads, and customers from SEO. Install Google analytics to your website to track how many visitors you are receiving and where are they coming from.

Once you have done some of these things to improve your website, it is recommended to have one of the free website graders on the internet score if your website to see where you can improve your search engine visibility.

**Here are some websites you can go to:**
www.websitegrader.com
www.reviewmyweb.com

Submit Your Website To The Search Engines:
Now that you have tuned up your website, you need to submit it to the search engines. Even if your website has been in the search engines before, you will need to resubmit it for the search engines to crawl and analyze your website. You should have your website submitted every month if possible.

There are literally billions of websites on the internet and you need to constantly submit to them to be found, also as you do the other tools in this guide you will watch your website start moving toward the first page of search results greatly increasing the amount of visitors you have on your website.

You can do this manually, however it does take time or you can pay someone to submit your site to multiple search engines for you. There are companies that do it freely in exchange for placing their link on your homepage.

**Here are a couple of companies you can use:**
www.google.com/addurl/

www.submitexpress.com/submit.html
www.addme.com
www.freewebsubmission.com

And there many more sites to submit your site to, just Google search submit my site to the search engines and you can find more companies.

**Get Found Online: Blogs**
What is a blog? A blog, or weblog, is a website that allows for regularly posted content or articles. Blogging is Inbound Marketing-Placing interesting content about you or your services out on the web where they will choose to find you. Blogging helps with SEO. Blogging helps with social news and networking sites. Blogging is permission centric.

**How To Get Found Online: Blogs**

1. Read other blogs that pertain to your area or real estate market, there are blogs so specific they even talk about specific housing tracts and events in the area.

Search for other blogs in your industry using Technorati.com or BlogSearch.Google.com.

Read and subscribe to blogs via RSS (Really Simple Syndication) or email – RSS allows users to subscribe anonymously and consume content however they want. It also records what you write and blog about and sends that to the search engines constantly.

2. Comment on other people's blogs.

Contribute to the conversation via a comment.

Increase the value of the article – share an example, add a point, add a useful link, disagree, ask a question. Why? When you engage to the community, then more and more people will read it and want to talk to you.

This is also a great way to create links back to your website and this will increase your website ranking and the amount of visitors to your website seeking your services.

**Add a Blog to Your Own Website**

You may want to provide tips and updates for your local real estate market on your blog, as we have said before; you can literally blog about almost anything. In every blog you do make sure to reference your own website and contact information.

**Try typing in real estate blogs in Google and you will be amazed at how many real estate blogs there are on the internet that you can blog on. Or once you learned how to blog, start your own blog-one good website is blogger.com.**

**Get Found Online: Social Media**

**What is social media?** Media (content that is published) with a social (anyone can add to and share it) component. Social media is like a business networking, reception without the constraints of time and space.

Social Media is Inbound Marketing Social media helps with SEO.

Social media promotes your blog. Social media is permission centric.

Some of the Top Social Media websites are Facebook, twitter, MySpace, LinkedIn, squidoo, and there are so many more. We are going to talk about Facebook, twitter, and MySpace but, do not stop there, there are literally millions of social networking sites out there. Join as many as you want to, the more you join the more it will increase the marketing of your services and your website to attack visitors.

**How you can use Twitter to Grow your Foreclosure Cleanup-Property Preservation Business**
http://www.twitter.com

**Here are some of the topics we are going to cover:**
What is Twitter?
Why is it valuable?
How does it work?
How should a business get started?
What does it make possible?

Your fears and concerns
And Much More…

## What is twitter?

**Twitter is a completely mobile way of interacting with a huge audience; you can interact through your mobile phone or on the internet. People type short messages, less than 140 characters about interesting topics and network between each other.**

**Why is it valuable? Brand your name out through tons of people at one time for free-twitter costs nothing but time!**

Twitter allows you to engage more deeply with consumers and markets in strategic and powerful ways.

## So what does Twitter do for businesses?

 Twitter is a communication platform that helps businesses stay connected to their customers.

As a business, you can use it to quickly share information with people interested in your company or using your services and build relationships with customers and other people who care about you or your company. As an individual user, you can use Twitter to tell a company (or anyone else) that you've had a great-or disappointing-experience with their business, offer product ideas, and learn about great offers.

## So how does it work?

Twitter lets you write and read messages of up to 140 characters or less in length, including all punctuation and spaces.  The messages are public and you decide what sort of messages you want to receive-Twitter being a recipient driven information network.  In addition, you can send and receive Twitter messages, or tweets, equally well from your desktop or your mobile phone.

## So how do businesses use Twitter?

Twitter connects you to your customers right now, in a way that was never before possible.

With twitter you can: Build your network fast, access better professional relationships, have faster knowledge-sharing!

Connect with Realtors, REO Agents, REO Asset Managers, and more...

**Value Twitter can be for you & your business:**
Visibility
Community
Customer Service
Relevance
Ideas
Trust
Drive Traffic to your website
Relationships
Marketing to your website
Social capital
Networking

**What's in it for you?**

 **INFLUENCE-Attracting attention to yourself and your website!!!**

**Before you post your first message**
Before you get started, it's important to understand that on Twitter, people choose to view your updates by searching for specific knowledge or by following your account.
This recipient-controlled model means that if you are compelling to people on Twitter, they'll choose to view your updates. The reverse is also true-people may choose to un-follow you just as easily.
Dry, boring feeds rarely draw many people. Successful Twitter business accounts, though, can take many forms. They may be personal and chatty or they might even have mostly automated information. But no matter the style, the key is to post messages that your followers will find compelling.

Tip: Help people understand what to expect from your Twitter account by posting a little description in your Bio.

So making your posts on Twitter interesting is key, but what are you going to post about? That depends on your goals. Do you want to build deeper relationships? Or do you want to provide more responsive and immediate customer service?

You can meet several communication goals simultaneously by thinking about your Twitter account as a friendly information booth or place to chat.

It's a place for people to ask you spontaneous questions of all kinds-a spot to share intriguing company insights they might find interesting. Tweeting often can help build valuable relationships.

Regardless of how you plan on using Twitter, you should figure out how to integrate it with your existing communication channels.

To get a sense of what Twitter can do for your business, spend a little time listening in on the conversations happening right now (you can use Twitter search whether or not you have an account).

Listening will help you quickly learn what people are saying about you or your company, and it will also give you a feel for the flow of conversations on Twitter. In addition, it can give you insight into how other companies handle Twitter exchanges.

Once you've got a sense of how you want to engage on Twitter, you're ready to dive in.

You want to add people to connect with on twitter for them to read your tweets, search realtors, real estate, real estate agents, real estate brokers, and more, then start fowling them-most people will immediately start following you also, then you're on your way to marketing to your select group of professionals you want to market to.

**Jump in and get started today!**

If you haven't yet signed up for an account, it's easy, and it takes just a few minutes. Here's how to get started:

**Sign up** Go to the sign up page, www.twitter.com and fill out the four fields. If you're creating a company account, use the "Full Name" field to type in your company name. That'll help people find your company or team on Twitter. (You can add your own name in the Bio field, as described below.) If you are not part of a real estate team, then I would recommend using your personal name, not your company's name.

The username is the name by which you'll be known on Twitter, for real estate professionals. I highly recommend this to be your name. This will promote your name more and more for people to remember you as a professional in their area and someone they can call on when they want to utilize your services or recommend you to someone.

After you've signed up, the site will walk you through a couple of screens to help you find people on Twitter you know or might be interested in.

**Fill Out Your Information**

Before you do anything else, click Settings to get a page where you can fill out a few more details to help people recognize your company. Most of the fields are self-explanatory.

But pay special attention to the Bio, which gives you quite a bit of space to write about yourself; this is a great place to list information about you and what you have to offer, always make sure to include your website, email information, and phone number, too.

Before you leave Settings, check out the Picture tab, you should definitely add a photo of yourself as this helps the other twitter people to easily remember and recognize you more. On the Design tab, you can upload a background image for your Twitter home page and change the page colors to your choice.

**Find Highly Relevant People And Companies To Follow**

Whether or not chose to follow anyone in the sign-up process, now's a good time to search for people and companies of specific interest to you. Use the search box on your Twitter home page to look not only for people talking about your company, brands and products, but also for partners and mentions of key terms in your sector.

When you find interesting messages, consider following those accounts. No need to worry about the number of people you're following-just follow a few whose updates you really want to read, say hello and let conversations grow. Go to the <u>Find People</u> section and type whatever search term you would like to enter to find people.

**Post Your First Message**

This is where the fun begins. On your Twitter home page, in the box at the top, it says "What are you doing?" Type in a message; whatever you would like to type in there. When you've finished typing what you want to say, hit Update to post it (pressing Enter won't do the trick). There you go, you've done it-you've send your first tweet.

If you chose to skip the step during setup of searching for people, you should do this now. People will not see your messages unless you have people following, add as many people and businesses as you would like, the more the better. People are very friendly on twitter and when you follow them, most of the time the start following you. Good luck and get tweeting!

**Twitter is a great way for real estate people to become well known in their area, take advantage of that!!**

**Real Estate and Facebook-How Facebook can help grow your business and connect you with potential clients** <u>http://www.facebook.com</u>

Facebook is another excellent website for networking for real estate professionals. Make sure your site that you use for your Facebook contains appropriate content as your website would. You will be able to connect with customers once you started networking.
**\*\*Facebook has more than 200 million active users registered and over 100 million users log on to it at least once a day!! If that isn't enough reason to get your business on Facebook, than I don't know what is!!**

**So Let's Get Started...**

First you will want to go to <u>www.facebook.com</u> and sign up; it only takes a few minutes. Then, create your profile if you don't have one already. Add your pictures and tell about yourself completely and include your website, email, and phone number so people can contact you. As a real estate professional, many people find you on Facebook but may want to call you and speak to you personally. Keep your Facebook professional as these are people you will want to business with. Next, you will want to connect with people you already know, you can import your email address book and it will tell you of other people that are already on Facebook that you can connect with.

## Now-Start Connecting With Huge Groups Of People

Many people are already on Facebook and do not know that Facebook has discussion areas, entire huge groups of people discussing different topics. Go to the search bar and type in discussions. An entire page will come up where you can search by people, pages, groups, and more.

Search out the people you would like to add. Then go back and search out real estate groups, investors, etc. Add as many as you can, because the more **people** and groups you add the more people you will be marketing to.

Now that you've added people and groups, these people will all see everything you add to your Facebook page and it will encourage them to come back to your site more often and see what you are up to.

## Create Your Own Blogs

I would highly recommend everyone to create blogs about yourself and the services you have to offer. You can literally blog about anything that is relevant to your business, area, market, or what you have to offer. Always reference your website, email, and contact information. Every time you do this you will be increasing your website in the search engines as there is more content about you out there! And it will be helping your website rank higher in the search engines with back links to your website.

## Facebook Classifieds

Facebook and Oodle are partnered together and will be offering classified ads; they have not actually come live with the new website; however we wanted to mention this because it should be arriving shortly. You will want to keep an eye out for it when it comes out and place ads offering your real estate services on them.

## Facebook Paid Ads

These are similar to Google adwords where you pay for the advertising; however they have very reasonable rates that I would not overlook this as a way of advertising.

Here is there link: http://www.facebook.com/advertising/

You can even specify your marketing ads to only show up in your geographical area and by the age of the users:

- Reach over 300,000,000 active Facebook users
- Attach social actions to your ads to increase relevance
- Create demand for your product with relevant ads

## Real Estate Marketing, Networking And MySpace
## Grow Your Business On MySpace
### http://www.myspace.com

**MySpace has nearly 130 million monthly active users around the globe; MySpace has more than 70 million total unique users in the US**

**MySpace was one of the first social media giants to grow to outstanding numbers, Facebook has actually surpassed MySpace, however you still have 70 million potential customers out there to market to!**

MySpace is all over the news and all over computer screens across America and beyond. In November of 2005, MySpace had 26.7 million users*. Just one year later, an estimated 128 million people were using MySpace, the site that according to Wikipedia "attracts new registrations at a rate of 230,000 per day". And although teens may appear to be more hip to MySpace lingo, an October 2006 report by comScore Media Matrix notes that "more than half of all MySpace visitors are now age 35 or older."

## Getting Started:

First go to www.myspace.com and register and set up your account and profile.  Once again, include your picture, website, email, phone number and what you have to offer your potential clients.

Next, search for friend, colleagues, former clients, and potential clients in the browse people search bar and send them friend requests so you can get connected to them.

**Events:**  You can post events such as open houses and more on the more tab, here's the link:
http://event.myspace.com/index.cfm?fuseaction=events

### FREE MySpace Advertising

You can even place banners and text ads in your specific area with my space.  Here is the link:
https//advertise.myspace.com/login.html?adv=gf.1&pr=d3oatQsvADw%2Bazsd1%2FiOA%3D%3D

You can run banner and text ads for as low as $5 a day and have them only advertise in the areas you want them to, and you can even target by age.  This is another great way to market your business and reach thousands to millions of potential customers.

### Google Adwords

Advertise your business on Google no matter what your budget, you can display your ads on Google and our advertising network.  Pay only if people click your ads.  You can set your own budget upon how much you want to spend, your geographical area, and more.  Go to: www.google.com and type in Google adwords to be taken to the signup page.

### Advertising Your Foreclosure Cleanup-Property Preservation Business On Craigslist:

### Http://www.craigslist.org/about/sites

Craigslist is a great place to offer your services that is absolutely free! You need to post almost daily, but millions of people look on craigslist every day! List your services in the Real Estate section, trash and hauling services, and more to attract realtors to use your services.

## Create Videos and Posting Them To MySpace, Facebook, and YouTube Offering Your Real Estate Services

Creating a video is relatively easy in this day and age; you can even to it from a lot of cell phones and post your video in minutes. Create videos advertising your expertise and what you have to offer and then upload your video to YouTube, MySpace, and Facebook with links back to your website so your potential customers can find you.

## Install An Auto-Responder For Your Email

When people go to your website and would like to contact via your website, they usually fill in their information and hit send. You will then receive the email, but as well know how every important we are, we may be sitting in front of the computer at the time it comes in. An email auto-responder will email them immediately letting them know that you will be contacting them shortly. Potential clients love this as they feel that you have responded to them immediately, it builds thrust and will help you secure those internet leads you receive.

## Publish Free Articles About Yourself, Your Area, And Your Community

Yu can actually create and publish free articles and submit them all over the web about yourself, your community and more.

# 7 BANKS AND REO ASSET MANAGEMENT CONTACT LIST

This list is great for anyone looking for a new, hot business or an outstanding way to expand their current business!  This list is wonderful for Contractors, Painters, Landscapers, Handyman, Appraisers or anyone looking to start a brand, new business venture.  This business can be extremely profitable! The work is everywhere from Coast to Coast!  Some Property Preservation companies say they have TOO much business to handle!

**Register with the Banks and REO Asset Management Companies-This is extremely crucial for your success in this business!**

**Welcome to the Booming Foreclosure Industry!**

The foreclosure vendors or independent contracts receive most work orders by internet sign in, fax, or through email.  So sign up with as many companies as you can and the business will just come to you!  The following list includes website links where you may sign up as a vendor with the bank or third party vendor.  99% of banks require potential vendors to sign up on these websites to start receiving work orders.  You usually will need a few items to sign up with them:
- Business License Number
- Contractor's License Number
- Workman's Compensation Insurance
- W-9 Signed by you as they pay you as an independent contractor
- Liability Insurance
- Business Contact Information such as Name, Phone
- Number, and Billing Address for your company

**Sign up with these companies as soon as possible, once the banks have you added as a current vendor in their database, work orders in your geographical area will start pouring in.**

1. 4REOBROKERS.COM (www.4reobrokers.com)
2. Asset Disposition Management, Inc. (www.admreo.com/buspartners.html)

3.  ASD America (www.asdamerica.com)
4.  Phoenix Asset Management, LLC (www.assetonemg.com/Website/index.html)
5.  Chase – If you are contractor interested in doing work for Chase, please send an email to REO.VENDOR@CHASE.COM to obtain further information.
6.  ClearCapital (www.clearcapital.com)
7.  Corporate Asset Management, LLC (www.camreo.com)
8.  Corporate Realty Service, LLC (www.crsreo.com/stlouis_register/stlouis_reo/missouri_reo)
9.  Field Assets Services, Inc. (www.fieldassets.com)
10. First American Field Services (www.firstam.com/field/html/cust/1400.html
11. Five Brothers Mortgage Company Services and Securing (www.fivebrms.com/vendor.php)
12. Fiserv (www.fiservlendingsolutions.com/requestform.aspx
13. Goodman Dean (www.goodmandean.com)
14. Integrated Asset Services (www.iasreo.com/contact.aspx)
15. Keystone Asset Management (www.keystonebest.com)
16. LandAmerica (www.nascopgh.com/vendorops.aspx)
17. Lenders Asset Management Corporation (www.lendersreo.com)
18. Lighthouse Real Estate Solutions (www.lrescorp.com/agents.htm)
19. LPS Field Services (www.fndfs.com/fs2/)
20. Michaelson, Connor, & Boul (www.mcbreo.com/contractors.htm)
21. National Default Servicing (www.defaultservicingllc.com/clients.htm)
22. National Field Representatives, Inc. (www.nationalfieldreps.com)
23. National Foreclosure Services (www.nationalforeclosureservices.com)
24. National REO (www.nreo.com/Content/Appraisal.aspx)
25. National Vendor Management Services (http://nvms.com/Register.aspx)
26. Network Mortgaging Servicing (www.networkmortgageservicing.com)
27. OCWEN (www.ora-rmsi.com/webtop/default.asp)
28. Pacific Field Service, Inc. (www.pacfield.com/contactus.aspx)
29. Premiere Asset Services (www.reosource.com)
30. Premier Field Services, LLC (www.premierfield.com/vendorapp.html)
31. Pro-Tek Valuation Services (www.protk.com/vendorsignup.asp)

32. Reliance Field Services (reliancefieldservices.com/preo.html)
33. REM Corporation
    (www.remusa.com/fieldreps/fieldrepssignupfieldrep.cfm)
34. REO America (www.reoam.com/reoservices.htm)
35. REO Solutions (www.resolutions.net)
36. REOTRANS (www.reotrans.com)
37. REO Nationwide (www.reonationwide.com/index.asp)
38. REO Network (www.reonetwork.com/apply/vendor_step_1.cfm)
39. Safeguard Properties (www.safeguardproperties.com)
40. Security National (https://bpo.snsc.com/login.aspx)
41. TREO - The REO Service Network (www.treonet.com/usa)
42. W-M Realty Services (www.w-mgroup.com/propertypreservationservices.aspx)

## ABOUT THE AUTHOR

The author is a Real Estate Contractor, Investor, and Foreclosure Cleanup Business owner. As a result, readers learn crucial start-up tactics from a real estate professional with pointed experience in several real estate industry capacities.